How We Got the Bible

Leader Guide

Timothy Paul Jones, PhD

Developed by Garrick Bailey

This Leader Guide accompanies the
How We Got the Bible 6-Session DVD-Based Study
(ISBN 9781628622072 or 9781628622065)
with
How We Got the Bible Participant Guide
(ISBN 9781628622126)

ROSE PUBLISHING

Carson, California

How We Got the Bible Leader Guide
Copyright ©2015 Bristol Works, Inc.
Rose Publishing, Inc.
17909 Adria Maru Lane
Carson, California 90746 USA
Email: info@rose-publishing.com
www.rose-publishing.com

Register your Rose Publishing books at www.rose-publishing.com/register.

This book is published in association with Nappaland Literary Agency, an independent agency dedicated to publishing works that are: Authentic. Relevant. Eternal. Visit us on the web at Nappaland.com.

Printed in the United States of America

Contents

About This Study

Have you ever had a coworker ask you about books that were supposedly cut out of the Bible? Or maybe somebody tried to tell you that the person who *really* chose the books of the Bible was the Emperor Constantine. Maybe you've heard words like "inerrant" and "infallible" and you wonder what exactly do we mean when we say that the Bible is inerrant and infallible.

In this six-session study on *How We Got the Bible* you'll learn about all these things, plus a lot more. You'll learn how the books in your Bible ended up there, and why we can trust the text of the Old and New Testaments. You'll learn how the Bible was copied and translated, and the fascinating stories of people in history who risked their lives to spread the Word of God.

This study is designed for six 60-minute sessions with the video portion lasting about 30 minutes. The teaching can be expanded to six 90-minute sessions by using the *How We Got the Bible* handbook, PowerPoint® and other materials included in the Complete Kit. Participant guides for class members contain group discussion questions, Bible study questions, session outlines for following along with the video and taking notes, and additional material for further learning.

About the Author

Timothy Paul Jones , PhD, serves as the C. Edwin Gheens Professor of Christian Ministry and as associate vice president at The Southern Baptist Theological Seminary, the flagship school of the Southern Baptist Convention and one of the largest seminaries in the world. Before coming to Southern Seminary, Dr. Jones led churches in Missouri and Oklahoma as a pastor and an associate pastor.

Dr. Jones has authored or coauthored more than a dozen books in the fields of family ministry and apologetics, including the CBA bestseller *The Da Vinci Codebreaker*. In 2007, Charles Colson listed him as one of "four names you need to know" when responding to the new atheists. Christian Retailing Magazine awarded Jones top honors in 2010 in the Christian education category for his book *Christian History Made Easy*. Jones has also received the Scholastic Recognition Award from the North American Professors of Christian Education for his research in faith development.

The son of a rural pastor, Dr. Jones earned his bachelor of arts degree in biblical studies at Manhattan Christian College. He also holds the Master of Divinity degree from Midwestern Baptist Theological Seminary and the Doctor of Philosophy degree from The Southern Baptist Theological Seminary. He has taught biblical languages at Midwestern Baptist Theological Seminary and at Oklahoma Baptist University, as well as lecturing on the reliability of the New Testament Gospels at the University of North Carolina (Chapel Hill) at forums sponsored by InterVarsity Christian Fellowship.

Despite his academic background, Dr. Jones has shown a capacity to communicate to ordinary people in an appealing and accessible style. He has been interviewed on numerous radio and television programs, including WGN Morning News, Fox & Friends, Crosstalk America, and Bible Answer Man. Dr. Jones is married to Rayann and they have three daughters.

Garrick Bailey (ThM, Dallas Theological Seminary) is a PhD student in Systematic Theology at The Southern Baptist Theological Seminary. His research interests include the theology of the early church and Roman Catholicism. He serves on the editorial staff for the Center for Ancient Christian Studies and the *Journal of Discipleship and Family Ministry*. When he's not reading or drinking coffee—usually at the same time—you will find him spending time with his wife and two children.

About the Complete Kit

How We Got the Bible Complete Kit (ISBN 9781628622072) contains everything you need to get started:

- DVD with six 30-minute video sessions.

- Leader Guide (printed copy plus a PDF for your iPad or tablet)

- Participant Guide (printed) with session outlines, discussion and study questions, and extra information. Buy additional participant guides for each class member (ISBN 9781628622126).

- Reference handbook, *How We Got the Bible*

- Fold-out time line of the history of the Bible

- Ready-to-use PowerPoint® presentation with 100+ slides to expand the scope of teaching

- CD-ROM with printable PDFs of promotional posters, banners, fliers, handouts, and bulletin inserts.

Available at www.HowWeGotTheBibleDVD.com or www.rose-publishing.com or by calling Rose Publishing at 1-800-532-4278. Also available wherever good Christian books are sold.

What's So Special about the Bible?

Get This: When Scripture speaks, God speaks.

"All Scripture is breathed out by God and profitable for teaching, for reproof, for correction, and for training in righteousness, that the man of God may be complete, equipped for every good work."—2 Timothy 3:16–17

Session 1 Outline

Use this session outline to follow along with the video and take notes.

1. The Bible is inspired.

    a. All Scripture is God-breathed (2 Timothy 3:14–16).

    b. Paul identifies a text that would become part of Luke's Gospel as Scripture (1 Timothy 5:18 and Luke 10:7).

    c. Peter identifies Paul's writings as Scripture (2 Peter 3:16).

    d. The authors wrote the words God intended, but in their own literary style.

2. The Bible is infallible and inerrant.

    a. Infallibility—The Bible is unable to deceive (John 10:35).

    b. Inerrancy—The Bible never errs.

3. The Bible is sufficient.

    a. Scripture *provides* what we need to know God.

    b. Scripture has been sufficiently *preserved*.

4. Scripture must transform us.

    a. Scripture is like a mirror (James 1:22–24).

    b. The Bible is dependent on *interpretation* and *illumination* for application (1 Peter 1:11).

Key Terms

Autographs—The original manuscripts of the Bible (from the Greek *autographos,* "written in one's own hand").

Illumination—The enlightening work of the Holy Spirit in the Christian person and community, enabling believers to understand and to obey the Scriptures.[1]

Inerrancy—The Bible is completely trustworthy and contains no errors in the original autographs.

Infallibility—The Bible is incapable of deceiving us and will never fail in its purpose of revealing God and the way of salvation to humans.

Inspiration—The work of the Holy Spirit enabling the human authors of the Bible to record what God desired to have written in the Scriptures.

Interpretation—Explanation of the intended meaning of a text. The study of interpretation is known as "hermeneutics," from the Greek *hermeneuo* ("I translate").

Manuscript—A text copied by hand rather than printed using a printer or printing press.

Sufficiency—Scripture is sufficient in two senses: First and foremost, Scripture provides enough knowledge for us to find God's truth and to live in fellowship with him. Second, Scripture has been copied with enough accuracy to preserve God's truth.

Before the Gathering

- Prayerfully seek God's guidance for this gathering.

- **Watch the video:** *Session 1: What's So Special about the Bible?* (30 minutes). You can use the *Session Outline* in this Leader Guide to take notes.

- **Read the book:** Chapter 1 of *How We Got the Bible* handbook (ISBN 9781628622164)

- **Consider the questions:** Review the group discussion questions provided in this Leader Guide and choose at least two questions that you want to ask during the discussion time. Also, spend some time considering the *Questions Participants May Ask* found in this Leader Guide. No person can be an expert on all topics or have the answers to all questions, but it might be beneficial to think through how you would respond to these possible questions.

- For this first session, we have provided an icebreaker game to help participants get to know one another, and also a short quiz to get them thinking about the topic of how we got the Bible. For the quiz, make a copy for each person, and be sure you have writing utensils for each participant. This same quiz will be given at the conclusion of *How We Got the Bible* study to encourage participants by helping them to recognize how much they have learned together after six weeks. If you don't have enough time in this first session, choose either to do the icebreaker or the quiz.

- If you are expanding the session to 90 minutes or longer (optional):

  ○ Study the key Bible passage: 2 Timothy 3:14–4:5. See the *Recommended Resources* in this Leader Guide for books to assist you in your study.

  ○ Review the *Study Questions.* (These same questions are also in class members' Participant Guides.)

  ○ If you are using the *How We Got the Bible* PowerPoint® to expand the teaching time, review the section *10 Key Points about the Bible* for a brief overview of the Bible.

- Set up and test audio and video equipment beforehand.

- Obtain a *How We Got the Bible* Participant Guide for every class member. (ISBN 9781628622126)

Gathering Together

Open the Session (15 MINUTES)

Get to Know the Group

In the spirit of the reliability and trustworthiness of Scripture and for the purpose of loosening the group up, we would like to introduce you to an enjoyable game called "Two Truths and a Lie."

Give the participants several minutes to think of two truthful claims (presumably facts that no one in the group knows about them) and one false claim about themselves. When everyone has done so, each participant will present all facts about themselves without revealing which ones are true and which ones are not. The group will then vote on which fact they believe to be false. You can play multiple rounds of this game or turn it into a weekly icebreaker where group members have to come up with new facts each time. Enjoy!

Get Them Thinking about the Study

Before beginning the *How We Got the Bible* study, consider giving the following short quiz. It will appear again at the end of Session 6 so that participants can see what they've learned. Perhaps you could read the questions out loud and collect participants' quizzes to compare with their answers after they retake the same quiz after the end of Session 6. Be sure to emphasize to participants that it's okay if they don't know any of the answers. That's what this six-week study is about: to learn all of these facts, and many more! Encourage them by telling them that, by the end of this study, they'll know so much more about how we got the Bible.

How We Got the Bible Quiz

1. How many books are in the Bible?

   _____

2. How many human authors wrote the books of the Bible?

   a. Fewer than 10
   b. Between 10 and 25
   c. At least 40
   d. More than 100

3. What do we call the original manuscripts of the Bible?

   _____

4. How many original manuscripts of the Bible survive today?

   _____

5. In what language(s) was the Old Testament originally written?

   _____

6. In what language was the New Testament originally written?

   _____

7. What do we call the ancient Greek translation of the Old Testament?

   _____

8. When did mass printing of Bibles begin?

   a. Before AD 300
   b. Around AD 650
   c. After AD 1400
   d. After AD 1750

9. How many ancient Greek manuscripts of the New Testament exist?

   a. Fewer than 1,000
   b. Between 1,000 and 2,500
   c. Between 2,500 and 5,000
   d. More than 5,000

10. Who is known as the "father of the English Bible"?

   _____

Answer Key:

(1) 66

(2) c. At least 40

(3) Autographs

(4) Zero. There are no surviving *original* manuscripts.

(5) Hebrew (and some portions in Aramaic)

(6) Greek (or Koine Greek)

(7) Septuagint (or LXX)

(8) c. After AD 1400 (Gutenberg Printing Press about AD 1450)

(9) d. More than 5,000

(10) William Tyndale (John Wycliffe could also be a correct response.)

Take a Closer Look (30 MINUTES)

Watch the video *Session 1: What's So Special about the Bible?* Inform class members that they can follow along and take notes on the session outlines in their Participant Guides.

Seek the Central Truth (30 MINUTES – OPTIONAL)

Key Bible Passage

Drawing from your personal study and from the study notes, guide participants in a discussion of 2 Timothy 3:14–4:5.

Study Notes:

> The word translated "breathed out by God" (some translations read "inspired by God") combines the Greek words for "God" (*theos*) and "breathed" (*pneo*). Before Paul used the word (*theopneustos*) in his letter to Timothy, it seems to have appeared nowhere else in all of ancient literature. Paul points to the writings—not merely to the human authors—as communicating God's own authoritative words. When Scripture speaks, God speaks.

> God has given us his written word so that we can know the truth that saves us and leads us to righteousness (2 Timothy 3:15–17).

> In light of the Bible's divine origin, authority, and sufficiency in leading to salvation, we are called to share God's Word with others (2 Timothy 4:1–2).

Study Questions:

1. Where in 2 Timothy 3:14–4:5 do you see the authority of Scripture taught?

   _____

   _____

   _____

2. Where do you see the sufficiency of Scripture taught?

   _____

   _____

   _____

3. Where do you see the divine origin of Scripture taught?

   _____

   _____

   _____

4. How about Scripture's capacity to transform us?

   _____

   _____

5. Read Romans 15:4 and 2 Peter 1:19–21. What do these verses tell us about the origin and purpose of Scripture?

   _____

   _____

PowerPoint® Presentation

Teach through the section *10 Key Points about the Bible.*

Get Them Talking (10 MINUTES)

Discuss at least two of these questions.

1. Why are the three truths regarding the Bible—inspiration, infallibility, and sufficiency—important? (Hint: Imagine if a believer or a church were to reject those three truths about the Bible. What kind of impact would that have on their Bible study, prayer, habits, and daily life?)

_____

_____

_____

_____

2. Scripture can act like a mirror, showing us the truth about ourselves and spurring us to be doers of the Word not just hearers (James 1:22–24). Describe a time when God's Word worked like a mirror in your life.

_____

_____

_____

_____

3. The apostle Paul tells Timothy to "preach the word; be ready in season and out of season; reprove, rebuke, exhort, with great patience and instruction" (2 Timothy 4:2). What might this pattern look like in your life?

_____

_____

_____

Wrap It Up (5 MINUTES)

Prayer for the Road

"Father in heaven, empower us through the Holy Spirit to run the race well, keep the faith, strive toward righteousness, which is Christ Jesus, and do the good works you have prepared for us and equipped us for. In the name of Jesus, we pray. Amen." (Based on 2 Timothy 3:16–4:8).

Application for Daily Life

Encourage participants to ask someone they know about their views of the Bible before the next gathering. This is not an exercise in defending the Bible, but instead an opportunity to understand how different people in our culture perceive the message of Scripture.

Encourage students to read *How We Got the Bible* handbook this week: "Chapter 1: What's So Special about the Bible?"

Questions Participants May Ask

Did early Christians really believe in the inerrancy of Scripture?

The earliest Christians never used the words "inerrancy" and "infallibility." From the earliest stages of Christian history, however, faithful church leaders treated Scripture as God's inerrant and infallible revelation. Here are a few examples:

- "You have searched the Scriptures, which are true and given by the Holy Spirit. You know that nothing unrighteous or counterfeit is written in them."—Clement of Rome, 1st century[2]

- "All Scripture, which has been given to us by God, [is] perfectly consistent. The parables harmonize with the passages that are plain; and statements with a clearer meaning serve to explain the parables."—Irenaeus of Lyons, 2nd century[3]

- "I am entirely convinced that no Scripture contradicts another." —Justin Martyr, 2nd century[4]

- "The statements of Holy Scripture will never contradict the truth." —Tertullian of Carthage, 3rd century[5]

- "It is the opinion of some that the Scriptures do not agree or that the God who gave them is false. But there is no disagreement at all. Far from it! The Father, who is truth, cannot lie."—Athanasius of Alexandria, 4th century[6]

- "I have learned to give respect and honor to the canonical books of Scripture. Regarding these books alone, I most firmly believe that their authors were completely free from error. If in these writings I am confused by anything which appears to me opposed to the truth, I do not hesitate to suppose that either the manuscript is faulty, or the translator has not caught the meaning of what was said, or I myself have failed to understand it."—Augustine of Hippo, 5th century[7]

How can we know whether our application of a text is a result of the Spirit's illumination?

The Holy Spirit is the Spirit of truth; any truth that comes from the Spirit originates with the Father and exalts the Son (John 15:26; 16:12–13). The Spirit of truth will never illumine an application of the text of Scripture that contradicts correct interpretation of the text.

Does God approve of everything that's described in Scripture? If the Bible describes something like slavery and never condemns it, does that mean it's okay?

Some things are described because they really happened—not because God approved them: Some things were rightly recorded by Scripture even when what happened wasn't right. The Bible describes slavery and polygamy, for example, not because these practices were part of God's desire for humanity but because these practices happened in the context of God's work to redeem humanity. Since all have sinned, any accurate and reliable history will include descriptions of sin. This does not mean, however, that God condoned wrongdoing. If God could condone or ignore sin, the death of Jesus on the cross would have been unnecessary!

Some things were cultural practices, and the way these practices are expressed has changed from their culture to our culture: Have you ever wondered why we no longer greet each other with a "holy kiss"? (Romans 16:16; 1 Corinthians 16:20; 2 Corinthians 13:12; 1 Thessalonians 5:26; 1 Peter 5:14). In time, this became known in the church's worship as "the kiss of peace," which was replaced by bowing to one another and eventually—in most Western cultures—by shaking hands. Today, the handshake has almost entirely replaced the holy kiss as a form of Christian greeting because it was the principle of honoring and expressing love to one another that was to be passed on and not necessarily the specific cultural expression.

Some things are fulfilled in Jesus: Some things promised, predicted, or practiced in the past have been fulfilled in Jesus Christ. Why don't Christians sacrifice animals, for example? Because Jesus' sacrificial death on the cross has put sinful people right with God. For those who have trusted in Jesus Christ as their Savior, the sin that fractured our relationship with God has been atoned; there is no longer any need for animal sacrifices that symbolize the death of Jesus on the cross. The Old Testament laws have been fulfilled through the life, death, and resurrection of Jesus.

Recommended Resources

The Message of 2 Timothy (Bible Speaks Today) by John Stott (IVP Academic, 1984)

Words of Life by Timothy Ward (IVP Academic, 2009)

Bible Overview (Rose Publishing, 2012)

"The Inerrancy of Scripture: The Fifty Years' War ... and Counting" by Albert Mohler (www.albertmohler.com/2010/08/16/the-inerrancy-of-scripture-the-fifty-years-war-and-counting)

Notes:

_____

_____

_____

_____

_____

_____

_____

_____

_____

_____

_____

_____

_____

How We Got the Old Testament

Get This: Jesus trusted the Old Testament; so should we.

"So Ezra the priest brought the Law before the assembly, both men and women and all who could understand what they heard. … And the ears of all the people were attentive to the Book of the Law."—Nehemiah 8:2–3

Session 2 Outline

Use this session outline to follow along with the video and take notes.

1. Do we need the Old Testament?

    a. Some stories can't be started in the center.

    b. The Old Testament is the first part of the story of Jesus.

2. Who wrote the Old Testament?

    a. God etched the Ten Commandments (Exodus 32:16).

    b. Moses was the human source of the Torah (Exodus 17:14; Mark 12:26).

    c. Kings were to keep a copy of God's law (Deuteronomy 17:18–20).

    d. Ezra the scribe wrote later parts of the Old Testament.

3. How were the books of the Old Testament arranged?

    a. Torah (Law)

    b. Prophets

    c.   Writings (Also called Psalms)

4.   How was the Old Testament written and copied?

    a.   Paleo-Hebrew, square-script Hebrew, Aramaic (Nehemiah 8:8)

    b.   Masoretic scribes (5th century AD)

    c.   Dead Sea Scrolls

5.   Which books belong in the Old Testament?

    a.   Canon

    b.   Septuagint (LXX)

    c.   Jerome did not consider the Apocrypha to be authoritative.

    d.   Augustine of Hippo disagreed and considered the Apocrypha to be authoritative.

    e.   Jesus didn't recognize the Apocrypha as God's Word (Luke 24:44; 11:51).

Key Terms

Apocrypha—The name given to a collection of books that were thought to contain "hidden" or "secret" truths (from the Greek *apokrypha,* "hidden"). The books of the Apocrypha are considered canonical by the Roman Catholic and Orthodox Churches but are not included in the Jewish or most Protestant Scriptures. The Apocrypha includes books such as 1 and 2 Maccabees and Wisdom of Solomon.[8]

Canon—(from Greek *kanon,* "measuring stick") Religious texts that are authoritative for members of that particular religion.[9] The canon of the Bible refers to the collection of books in the Bible recognized as the authoritative Word of God.

Codex—The "book" form of ancient manuscripts, made up of a number of sheets of papyrus or parchment stacked and bound by fixing one edge (from Latin *caudex,* "block"). The codex was sometimes used by the Romans for business and legal transactions. Early Christians gathered the New Testament books in codex form.

Dead Sea Scrolls—Collection of more than 900 manuscripts (mostly in fragments) discovered by shepherds in 1947 in caves near the Dead Sea. These scrolls include portions or complete texts of all the books of the Old Testament except Esther, as well as many nonbiblical texts. The scrolls have assisted scholars in understanding the form of the text of the Hebrew and Aramaic Bible centuries before the Masoretic Text.[10]

Jerome (c. AD 345–420)—Prolific scholar of the early church. His greatest achievement was translating Scripture from the original languages into Latin (called the Vulgate). He advocated the acceptance of the Hebrew and Aramaic canon of Scripture by the Church, thereby excluding the books that came to be called "Apocrypha."[11]

Ketuvim (Writings)—The third section of the Hebrew canon, the Writings (sometimes known by its Latin name, *hagiographa*). The books in this section are Psalms, Job, Proverbs, Ruth, Song of Solomon (Song of Songs), Ecclesiastes, Lamentations, Esther, Daniel, Ezra, Nehemiah and 1 and 2 Chronicles.[12]

Masoretes—Copyists who preserved the traditional text of the Hebrew beginning as early as the 5th or 6th century AD. The most famous Masoretes were the Ben Asher family who copied the oldest surviving Old Testament codexes.[13] The text preserved by the Masoretes is known as the Masoretic Text.

Neviim (Prophets)—The second part of the Hebrew canon, including the Former and Latter Prophets. The Former Prophets include Joshua, Judges, 1 and 2 Samuel, 1 and 2 Kings. The Latter Prophets are Isaiah, Jeremiah, Ezekiel and the Twelve (Hosea, Joel, Amos, Obadiah, Jonah, Micah, Nahum, Habakkuk, Zephaniah, Haggai, Zechariah, Malachi).[14]

Old Testament—The first part of the Christian Bible, which tells the story of God's work with the descendants of Abraham and points forward to the New Testament fulfillment of this story in Jesus. The Old Testament was written primarily in Hebrew, with a few portions preserved in a related language known as Aramaic. "Testament" translates a Greek word that could also be rendered "covenant" (2 Corinthians 3:14; Hebrews 8:13). Also known as the Hebrew Scriptures, the Jewish Scriptures, or the First Testament.

Septuagint—Greek translation of the Hebrew Bible. This Greek translation was undertaken by the Greek-speaking Jews in Alexandria from the 3rd to the 2nd century BC. Later legend claimed that seventy-two Jewish scholars completed the translation in seventy-two days, working separately by invitation from Ptolemy II Philadelphus (285–246 BC). *Septuagint* comes from the Latin term for "seventy," and the abbreviation LXX is the Roman numeral for seventy.[15]

Tanak (also TNK, Tanakh)—Acronym for the Hebrew Scriptures: Torah (Law), Neviim (Prophets), Ketuvim (Writings).

Torah (Law)—The first part of the Hebrew canon, also known as the Pentateuch. The books in the Torah are Genesis, Exodus, Leviticus, Numbers, and Deuteronomy. Torah is sometimes translated "law." "The Law and the Prophets" could occasionally be used to refer to the Old Testament as a whole.

Before the Gathering

- Prayerfully seek God's guidance for this gathering.

- **Watch the video:** *Session 2: How We Got the Old Testament* (30 minutes)

- **Read the book:** Chapters 2 and 3 of *How We Got the Bible* handbook

- **Consider the questions:** Review the group discussion questions provided in this Leader Guide and choose 2 or 3 questions. Also, spend some time considering the *Questions Participants May Ask.*

- If you plan to do the activity in *Open the Session,* obtain three or more Bibles for this activity to get class members thinking about the topic.

- If you are expanding the session (optional):

  ◦ Study the key Bible passage: Nehemiah 7:73–8:18

  ◦ Review the participant study questions—also provided here in the Leader Guide.

  ◦ If you are using the PowerPoint® presentation, review the slides about the Old Testament, the Apocrypha, and the Dead Sea Scrolls.

- Set up and test audio and video equipment beforehand.

Gathering Together

Open the Session (5 MINUTES)

To open this session, bring three different Bible versions with you:

- One with the Apocrypha (New Jerusalem Bible, New American Bible),

- One without the Apocrypha (New International Version, New American Standard Version, English Standard Version, etc.),

- And a Jewish Bible ("The Complete Jewish Bible," "Jewish Study Bible").

To compare the differences, have three volunteers each take one of the Bibles and count the number of books in the Old Testament table of contents, and also note which books in their Bible begin and end the Old Testament. (Remember that in the Jewish Bible, it won't be called "Old Testament"; just have that volunteer count all the biblical books in the table of contents.) The differences will quickly be apparent. Explain to the class that in this session we'll learn why these Bibles are different.

Take a Closer Look (30 MINUTES)

Watch the video *Session 2: How We Got the Old Testament*

Seek the Central Truth (30 MINUTES - Optional)

Key Bible Passage

Drawing from your personal study and from the study notes, guide participants in a discussion of Nehemiah 7:73–8:18.

Study Notes:

> The "people" are the key characters in this passage as the word occurs sixteen times in 7:73–8:18. In eleven of those occurrences, "all the people" are mentioned. It seems that Ezra's role in this passage is reading the book, but the focus is on the people and their reaction to hearing the reading of the Law. The emphasis in this passage is on the people's response to hearing God's word. Their attentiveness (8:3), posture of respect (8:5), worship (8:6), posture of submission (8:6), and their repentance (8:9) display the proper reaction of the believer upon encountering God through the Scriptures.

One commentator reminds us:

> "The Word of God, when read, has the power to transform lives today just as it had in the time of both Josiah and Ezra. The Bible convicts, changes, and guides lives. In the time of Ezra the people realized that the Babylonian captivity was a result of disobedience. Only genuine repentance before God could bring about a real change in the community. The living power of the Word of God still liberates people from their own various forms of captivity. Leaders pointed out God's mercy to the people. Those who teach must show God's justice and the need for repentance but must not forget to emphasize God's love and mercy."[16]

Sin is any offense or rebellion against God. When we are confronted with our own offenses, we are filled with sorrow in the face of God's holiness and goodness. In 8:9–12, the people experienced these exact feelings, but Nehemiah and Ezra implored them to rejoice and celebrate because (1) they had heard and responded to God's Word, and (2) this was a day to celebrate God's deliverance (Leviticus 23:23–25; Deuteronomy 16:15).

Study Questions:

1. What does Nehemiah 8 tell us about the reverence and seriousness of the people as they received the Word of God?

_____

_____

_____

2. Who is included in the assembly of people throughout 7:73–8:18?

_____

_____

_____

3. Throughout the passage, we see the different reactions and emotions of mourning, sorrow, and rejoicing. What were the different reasons for this?

_____

_____

_____

PowerPoint® Presentation

Teach through the slides about the Old Testament, the Apocrypha, and the Dead Sea Scrolls.

Get Them Talking (20 MINUTES)

Discuss two or more of these questions.

1. If you stopped studying the Old Testament, how would that change your prayer, worship, and how you think about God?

_____

_____

_____

2. Read Isaiah 40:8, Matthew 5:18, and Mark 13:31. Do these passages give you confidence that God has preserved his Word throughout time? How can this confidence change the way you read your Bible?

_____

_____

_____

3. Another name for the Old Testament is the "old covenant." Covenants in the Bible are agreements and promises between two parties. The Old Testament tells the story of God's covenants with Israel and its authors looked forward to the "new covenant" or "new testament" that would be fulfilled in Jesus Christ (Jeremiah 31:31–32; Luke 22:20; 1 Corinthians 11:25; 2 Corinthians 3:6; Hebrews 8:1–13; 9:15; 12:24). When you consider how God has kept his promises—his covenants—how is your trust in him and the reliability of his Word affected? How would strengthened trust in God and his promises help you in your life right now?

_____

_____

_____

Wrap It Up (5 MINUTES)

Prayer for the Road

"Father in heaven, may your Word never depart from our hearts and lips. If we ever find ourselves wandering in the wilderness of disobedience, bring us back quickly Lord to repentance and rejoicing at the sound of your voice through your written Word."

Application for Daily Life

Pray for yourselves and your church that you would have a greater passion and confidence in God's Word. Ask that God would reveal areas of disobedience in your life and seek out at least one person who can walk alongside you as you seek to repent and live according to God's Word.

Encourage students to read *How We Got the Bible* handbook this week: "How We Got the Old Testament," "Chapter 2: How Did the Old Testament Get from God to You?" and "Chapter 3: Which Books Belong in the Old Testament?"

Questions Participants May Ask

Is the Old Testament really necessary for Christians?

Jesus treated the Old Testament as "the word of God" (Mark 7:13; see also Matthew 22:31–32; John 10:35). Jesus criticized the religious leaders' misuse of his Father's words—but he never corrected or contradicted the Old Testament laws and prophecies. Instead, he fulfilled them, and he treated them as the unerring revelation of his Father's will. The earliest Christians revered the Old Testament as God's Word because their Savior had recognized the Old Testament as God's Word. Sure, there are discontinuities between the Old Testament and the New Testament. That's because God's fulfillment of his promises in Jesus Christ inaugurated the kingdom that the Old Testament merely foreshadowed. But there's also unmistakable continuity between the two testaments, because the same God was fulfilling the same promises in both testaments. The Creator God who inspired the Old Testament was also the heavenly Father who sent his Son to be the Savior of the world.

How do we know the apocryphal writings aren't inspired?

A long line of Christians throughout history have concluded that the apocryphal writings were not God-breathed for three simple reasons:

1. The authors of the New Testament never quoted the Apocrypha as Scripture. The New Testament writers frequently used phrases like "it is written" or "Scripture says" when quoting Old Testament Scripture (for examples, see John 19:37; Romans 3:10; 1 Peter 2:6; Hebrews 3:7). Yet no New Testament author ever applied any of these clauses to any apocryphal text.

2. The Jewish people never recognized the Apocrypha as Scripture. According to the first-century Jewish historian Josephus, the Jews did not consider these later writings "of equal value" with Scripture because of "the failure of the exact succession of the prophets." In other words, even in the first and second centuries AD, Jews knew that the time of inspired prophecy had ended with the Hebrew and Aramaic texts in the Law, Prophets, and Writings.

3. Jesus recognized the three-part Hebrew and Aramaic canon as Scripture. The Scriptures that Jesus recognized were segmented into Law, Prophets, and other Writings (Luke 24:44)—and only the Hebrew and Aramaic canon is arranged into these three segments.

Recommended Resources

Ezra, Nehemiah, Esther (*The New American Commentary*) by Mervin Breneman (Broadman & Holman, 1993)

The Old Testament Documents: Are They Reliable & Relevant? by Walter C. Kaiser Jr. (IVP Academic, 2001)

Dead Sea Scrolls pamphlet by Randall Price (Rose Publishing, 2005)

The Digital Dead Sea Scrolls (http://dss.collections.imj.org.il)

Notes:

_____

_____

_____

_____

_____

_____

_____

_____

_____

_____

_____

_____

_____

_____

How We Got the New Testament

Get This: The testimony in the New Testament is trustworthy.

"For I delivered to you as of first importance what I also received: that Christ died for our sins in accordance with the Scriptures, that he was buried, that he was raised on the third day in accordance with the Scriptures, and that he appeared to Cephas, then to the twelve. Then he appeared to more than five hundred brothers at one time, most of whom are still alive, though some have fallen asleep."—1 Corinthians 15:3–6

Session 3 Outline

Use this session outline to follow along with the video and take notes.

1. When was the New Testament written?

    a. Paul's letter to the Galatians (AD 49)

    b. 1 and 2 Thessalonians (early AD 50s)

2. Oral histories of Jesus

    a. Stories were shared in a culture of memorization.

    b. Believers cared deeply about preserving the message of eyewitnesses.

        i. Luke (Luke 1:2)

        ii. Papias (1st century AD)

        iii. Pastor disciplined for fabricating stories about Paul in "Acts of Paul" (AD 160)

    c. Oral histories were written down before eyewitnesses passed away (1 Corinthians 15:3–8).

3. Why did Christians write the New Testament texts?

    a. Letters to address specific issues in churches

    b. Loss of eyewitnesses

4. The four Gospels

    a. Mark was the apostle Peter's translator.

    b. Matthew likely wrote in Aramaic; translated into Greek.

    c. Luke investigated and got stories from eyewitnesses.

    d. John was an eyewitness.

Key Terms

Autographs—The original manuscripts of the Bible in their final form are known as the *autographs*. The autographs of the New Testament decayed into dust centuries ago—but there is some evidence that the autographs might have survived at least until the end of the second century.

Gospel—(from Old English *godspel,* translation of Greek *euangelion,* "good news")

(1) gospel: Outside the New Testament in the first century AD, the word translated "gospel" referred to the proclamation of an event—such as a victory in battle or the rise of a new king—that changed the hearer's status and called for a response. In the New Testament, "gospel" came to mean the proclamation that the power of God's kingdom had entered human history through Jesus Christ to renew the whole world by means of his perfect life, substitutionary death, and victorious resurrection. When we trust what Jesus did—instead of what we can do—to be made right with God, God restores us to union with himself and communion with others.[17]

(2) Gospel: A text that narrates the life, death, and resurrection of Jesus Christ. The four New Testament Gospels—Matthew, Mark, Luke, and John—are ancient biographies (Greek, *bioi*) and were clearly intended to be read as historical testimonies.[18]

New Testament—The second part of the Christian Bible, which announces the fulfillment of God's Old Testament promises and the arrival of God's kingdom on earth through the perfect life, sacrificial death, and triumphant resurrection of Jesus Christ. The New Testament was originally written in Greek. "Testament" translates a Greek word that can also be rendered "covenant" (Luke 22:20; Hebrews 8:8–13).

Oral Culture—A culture in which stories and memories are recalled and shared primarily through spoken words instead of written words. In the oral culture of the first Christians, rhythmic patterns and mnemonic devices were woven into oral histories so that learners could quickly convert spoken testimonies into permanent memories. God worked through this cultural pattern to preserve the truths that we read today in the New Testament.

Oral Histories—Spoken testimonies which were memorized and shared in communities during the lifetimes of the eyewitnesses.

Before the Gathering

- Prayerfully seek God's guidance for this gathering.

- **Watch the video:** *Session 3: How We Got the New Testament* (30 minutes)

- **Read the book:** Chapter 4 of *How We Got the Bible* handbook

- **Consider the questions:** Review the group discussion questions provided in this Leader Guide and choose 2 or 3 questions. Also, spend some time considering the *Questions Participants May Ask*.

- If you will be playing the Telephone Game with your group to open this session, decide on and locate one or two "messages" to use in this activity. (See *Open the Session* for ideas.)

- If you are expanding the session (optional):

  ○ Study the key Bible passage: 1 Corinthians 15:1–11

  ○ Review the participant study questions—also provided here in the Leader Guide.

  ○ If you are using the PowerPoint® presentation, review the slides about Jesus and the New Testament writers.

- Set up and test audio and video equipment beforehand.

Gathering Together

Open the Session (10 MINUTES)

Play a quick round of the Telephone Game. If the class is too large, break into groups of 6–10 people. Have the group sit in a circle and you whisper a "message" to the first person. The first person then whispers it to the next person in the circle as best as he or she can remember it, then that person whispers it to the next, and so on until the message makes it back to the first person.

The message should be something difficult to remember, like an unfamiliar passage in the Old Testament (such as 1 Chronicles 7:1–2, 1 Kings 7:40–42, or Micah 2:12–13) or an obscure tongue twister (such as "Pretty Kitty Creighton" or "There was a Young Fisher"). This activity will demonstrate how in our culture where we write or record our messages word for word, it's difficult to pass on information verbally without it getting changed.

If you have time, play it again, but this time with a familiar Bible verse (like John 3:16 or Psalm 23:1) or a well-known tongue twister or rhyme (such as "Humpty Dumpty" or "I scream, you scream, we all scream for ice cream"). If the message makes it around the circle intact (or mostly!) that will demonstrate how something that has been committed to memory or is very familiar to a group can be passed on.

You should also note very clearly that even though the message got changed—a little or a lot—the person who started the message (you) is still here to set straight what the message actually should be. (The importance of this will be apparent after watching the video session.)

Take a Closer Look (30 MINUTES)

Watch the video *Session 3: How We Got the New Testament*

Seek the Central Truth (30 MINUTES - OPTIONAL)

Key Bible Passage

Drawing from your personal study and from the study notes, guide participants in a discussion of 1 Corinthians 15:1–11.

Study Notes:

Sixteenth-century church reformer Martin Luther claimed that if anyone rejects the resurrection of Jesus, "he must deny in a lump the Gospel and everything that is proclaimed of Christ and of God. For all of this is linked together like a chain. . . . Whoever denies this article must simultaneously deny far more . . . that God is God."[19]

"The resurrection is and always has been the foundation of all preaching about Christ. Without it, the gospel dwindles into an inspiring story of a wise teacher who suffered heroically as a victim of human perfidy. Paul hints that if they deviate from this belief, it brings their salvation into question."[20]

The Greek verb *koimao* in 15:6 literally means "sleep," but it is often used in the Bible to suggest death, especially when speaking of believers. The term "sleep" as a metaphor emphasizes the hope of resurrection: in the future, Christians will "wake up" from death.

The phrase, "resurrection of the dead" (one might also translate this phrase as "the standing of dead ones") meant just that! The notion of a spiritual (non-physical) resurrection—an idea that appeals to so many today—would have been incomprehensible to first-century Jews.[21]

Notice that Paul does not argue for the reality of Jesus' resurrection here; he assumes it for the purpose of a larger argument. How did Paul know the event was indeed real? It was part of the eyewitness testimony he received after (or at the time of) his conversion (15:3). "Paul establishes that it was something he received and passed on to them like a baton. He stresses the continuity of tradition. 'Among the first things' means 'the most important things,' or 'things of first importance.' What was first in importance was also probably spoken first."[22]

To drive home the point about the reliability of Paul's claim, see 1 Corinthians 15:5–8, where he points any potential resurrection doubters in the direction of countless eye witnesses who were still alive. The central claim of the New Testament is that Jesus was physically resurrected after being crucified. If this claim grew from decades of embellishment instead of historical truth, Jesus is dead, the apostles were liars, and our faith is vain (1 Corinthians 15:14–17). But evidences from the first and second centuries AD reveal that eyewitness testimony about Jesus emerged rapidly and circulated reliably. The New Testament texts relied on testimonies from apostolic eyewitnesses, and all of these texts were completed while the eyewitnesses were still alive.

Study Questions:

1. What are the essential truths of the gospel message as told by Paul in 1 Corinthians 15:1–11?

   _____

   _____

   _____

2. What assurances does Paul give the church in Corinth on the basis of the resurrection of Jesus?

   _____

   _____

   _____

3. In your own words, what is Paul's main point that he wants to emphasize to the believers in Corinth in verse 11?

   _____

   _____

   _____

PowerPoint® Presentation

Teach through the slides about Jesus and the New Testament writers.

Get Them Talking (15 MINUTES)

Discuss two or more of these questions.

1. Compared to other ancient historical writings, the New Testament books were written not long after the events they describe— during the lifetime of eyewitnesses, in fact! Why do you think these eyewitness accounts are criticized and mistrusted by secular historians, even though other ancient eyewitness testimonies are accepted without question?

   _____

   _____

   _____

   _____

2. The Gospel is historically trustworthy. How does this truth impact your everyday life?

   _____

   _____

   _____

   _____

3. Early Christians cared deeply about preserving and passing on the message of the eyewitnesses. Does your own life reflect that same passion? What are some things you can do to help more people hear or read this message?

   _____

   _____

   _____

   _____

Wrap It Up (5 MINUTES)

Prayer for the Road

"Father in heaven, thank you for sending your Son, the Word in flesh, and giving us Scripture, your Word written down. Help its truthfulness impact every aspect of our lives. Amen."

Application for Daily Life

As a group, commit to helping each other memorize 1 Corinthians 15:1–4 in order to communicate the gospel clearly when the opportunity arises. Give each class member a printed card or slip of paper with this Bible passage on it so they can put it somewhere where they'll see it often. Pray as a group for God to provide opportunities for sharing the gospel.

Encourage students to read *How We Got the Bible* handbook this week: "How We Got the New Testament" and "Chapter 4: Can We Trust the New Testament?"

Questions Participants May Ask

Were the oral histories about Jesus "modified, amplified, and embellished" over the years?

Not even close. Evidence from the first century AD shows that testimonies about Jesus remained remarkably stable as they spread across the Roman Empire. Yes, two decades stand between Jesus' death and the earliest surviving records about him—but that doesn't mean that testimonies about Jesus were somehow mangled beyond recovery. There is clear evidence in Paul's letters that the New Testament authors repeated and wrote the same testimonies they received. When they composed letters and Gospels, these authors drew from oral testimonies and teachings of eyewitnesses. Sometimes, they recited exact testimonies that their readers already knew (1 Corinthians 11:23–25; 15:3–7). Other times, they applied Jesus' teachings without quoting them word-for-word (Romans 14:14; 1 Corinthians 7:10–11; 9:14)—but there's no proof that the authors of the New Testament fabricated the words and works of Jesus.

What happened to the original manuscripts?

The original manuscripts of the Bible in their final form are known as the *autographs.* The autographs of the New Testament decayed into dust decades ago—but there is some evidence that the autographs survived at least until the end of the second century. Around AD 180, Tertullian of Carthage wrote, "You who are ready to exercise your curiosity, ... run over to the apostolic churches...where their own authentic writings are read."[23] "Authentic writings" might refer to the original documents sent by apostles—especially since Tertullian follows this statement by listing the specific cities where the first-century apostles sent their epistles.

Recommended Resources

1 Corinthians (*Baker Exegetical Commentary on the New Testament*) by David E. Garland (Baker, 2003)

From Text to Translation by Paul Wegner (Grand Rapids: Baker Academic, 2005)

Misquoting Truth by Timothy Paul Jones (InterVarsity Press, 2007)

"Beyond the Bible, what historical proofs do we have about the life of Jesus?" by Timothy Paul Jones (www.godtube.com/watch/?v=0JE2EFNU)

"What are the Gnostic Gospels?" by Timothy Paul Jones (www.godtube. com/watch/?v=WDGPG7NX)

Notes:

Notes:

_____

_____

_____

_____

_____

_____

_____

_____

_____

_____

_____

_____

_____

_____

_____

_____

_____

_____

How the Books of the New Testament Were Chosen

Get This: God created the New Testament canon by inspiring the written words of Christ-commissioned eyewitnesses and their close associates.

"And count the patience of our Lord as salvation, just as our beloved brother Paul also wrote to you according to the wisdom given him, as he does in all his letters when he speaks in them of these matters. There are some things in them that are hard to understand, which the ignorant and unstable twist to their own destruction, as they do the other Scriptures."—2 Peter 3:15–16

Session 4 Outline

1. Who created the canon of the New Testament?

Use this session outline to follow along with the video and take notes.

    a. The canon wasn't created by any human being.

    b. Early Christians recognized a canon that God had already created.

2. First-century Christians recognized the writings of Christ-commissioned apostles and their close associates as authoritative.

    a. Paul: Galatians 1:1; 1 Corinthians 14:37–38

    b. Peter: 2 Peter 3:15–16

    c. Gospel writers: Luke 1:1–2; John 21:24

    d. The Muratorian Fragment: "The Shepherd" was rejected as authoritative because it was written long after the time of the apostles.

3. Did all Christians recognize the same books?

   a. 20 books of the New Testament were always recognized; 7 books questioned.

   b. "Gospel of Peter" was rejected because it was not written by Peter.

4. Some New Testament books were questioned, but later it became clear that they could be traced to Christ-commissioned eyewitnesses and their close associates.

   a. Hebrews (See Hebrews 13:23)

   b. James and Jude were half-brothers of Jesus who saw the resurrected Christ.

   c. 1 and 2 Peter, 2 and 3 John were written by eyewitnesses of Jesus.

Key Terms

Apostle—From Greek *apostolos*, "sent out," "commissioned"; a witness of the resurrection of Jesus Christ (Acts 1:22) and recipient of his teachings (Ephesians 3:5), commissioned to safeguard the gospel and to apply the teachings of Jesus in the churches. Occasionally applied more broadly to individuals sent on a mission (Acts 14:4, 14).

Athanasius (c. 296–373)—A bishop in Alexandria who championed the doctrine of the Trinity against the heretic Arius. He wrote an Easter letter in the year AD 367 which listed the same 27 books that appear in the New Testament today.

Irenaeus (c. 130–c. 200)—As a pastor seeking to care for his people, Irenaeus came into sharp dispute with certain Gnostics who denied Christ's humanity. Around AD 180, Irenaeus wrote *Against Heresies* in which he mentioned all four Gospels in order along with their origins.

Lost Gospels—The term "lost Gospels" usually refers to ancient writings that were excluded from the New Testament, even though they included supposed recollections of events and teachings from the life of Jesus. Complete manuscripts of a few of these lost Gospels have survived. Others survive only in tiny fragments of papyrus or in brief quotations found in the writings of early Christian scholars. Several lost Gospels were discovered anew in the past 100 years. Copies of some texts—such as *Gospel of Philip, Gospel of Thomas, Gospel of Truth,* and *Coptic Gospel of the Egyptians*—were unearthed in 1945 in Egypt, near a village known as Nag Hammadi. If a *Gospel* is defined as an ancient retelling of the events or teachings from Jesus' life, there are fewer than 30 known Gospels. Unlike the New Testament Gospels, many lost Gospels record only isolated teachings or fragmentary incidents from the life of Jesus.

Muratorian Fragment—First known listing of Christian writings that were received as authoritative and be publicly read in the churches; so called because it's recorded on a fragment discovered by a man named Ludovico Muratori around 1740. No one knows who recorded this list; the list seems to have been written in the vicinity of Rome in the second half of the second century and may have originated in a gathering of church leaders. The list includes all the books that appear in the New Testament today except Hebrews, James, 1 and 2 Peter, and 2 and 3 John.

Before the Gathering

- Prayerfully seek God's guidance for this gathering.

- **Watch the video:** *Session 4: How the Books of the New Testament Were Chosen* (30 minutes)

- **Read the book:** Chapter 5 of *How We Got the Bible* handbook

- **Consider the questions:** Review the group discussion questions provided in this Leader Guide and choose 2 or 3 questions. Also, spend some time considering the *Questions Participants May Ask.*

- See *Open the Session* for an idea about how to get class members thinking about the topic.

- If you are expanding the session (optional):

  ◦ Study the key Bible passage: 2 Peter 1:1–2; 3:14–18

  ◦ Review the participant study questions—also provided here in the Leader Guide.

  ◦ If you are using the PowerPoint® presentation, review the slides about the books of the New Testament.

- Set up and test audio and video equipment beforehand.

Gathering Together

Open the Session (5 MINUTES)

Start the session with a teaser. Say to your group, did you know that ...?

- Jesus is actually the reincarnation of Seth, Adam and Eve's third son. [*Coptic Gospel of the Egyptians*]

- Jesus, as a boy, cursed another boy when he accidentally bumped into him. The boy died, and when the neighbors complained to Jesus' parents, Jesus used his miraculous powers to strike the neighbors blind. [*Gospel of Thomas*]

- Judas Iscariot was not a betrayer, but a hero to whom Jesus revealed the secrets of the universe—the only one of the disciples to truly understand Jesus. [*Gospel of Judas*]

Then explain: No, of course none of this is true. But these stories about Jesus are found in writings in the early centuries of Christianity. So why didn't these writings end up as part of the New Testament? That's what we'll learn in this session on the canon of the New Testament.

Take a Closer Look (30 MINUTES)

Watch the video *Session 4: How the Books of the New Testament Were Chosen*

Seek the Central Truth (30 MINUTES - OPTIONAL)

Key Bible Passage

Drawing from your personal study and from the study notes, guide participants in a discussion of 2 Peter 1:1–2; 3:14–18.

Study Notes:

> Peter was one of the twelve original apostles and was an eyewitness to everything Scripture tells us about Jesus' ministry, death, resurrection, and ascension. Not only was he an apostle, but he was also one of Christ's closest friends and a leader of the early church after Jesus returned to the Father.
>
> "Faith" (1:1) can refer to trust in and commitment to Jesus Christ, or to a body of authoritative teaching, or else, to the Christian faith as a religious movement.[24] In light of this translation issue, we could translate "To those who have obtained a faith" as "To you who have received the

true doctrine about Jesus Christ," or "To you who God has caused to trust in Jesus Christ."[25]

"Our beloved brother" (3:15): Paul was Peter's "beloved brother," that is, a coworker in the gospel and fellow believer. Paul is also "our" brother, suggesting that Paul was a fellow worker and fellow apostle with Peter. Paul himself often emphasized that his apostolic calling was given by God (Romans 12:3; 15:15; 1 Corinthians 3:10; Galatians 2:9; Ephesians 3:2, 7; Colossians 1:25); Peter clearly agreed.[26]

"According to the wisdom given him" (3:15): God was the source of Paul's wisdom.[27]

"Ignorant" (3:16) translates a word used nowhere else in the New Testament. It means not simply ignorant but "unlearned," "uneducated," "uninstructed," and is used primarily of people who have not received sufficient instruction in the interpretation of Scripture and are therefore prone to error. "Unstable" on the other hand describes those who are not firmly rooted in the teachings of the Christian faith and are therefore easily misled. The same word is used in 2:14, where it is translated as "unsteady."[28]

Study Questions:

1. What reasons did Peter give his readers to pay attention to this writing?

   _____

   _____

2. What do these words from Peter imply about Paul?

   _____

   _____

3. How does Peter describe the error of false teachers? How does Peter encourage his readers to combat these teachings?

   _____

   _____

PowerPoint® Presentation

Teach through the slides about the books of the New Testament.

Get Them Talking (20 MINUTES)

Discuss two or more of these questions.

1. Why is it important to say that early Christians *recognized* the canon of Scripture instead of *created* it? What beliefs about God and his Word are we communicating by saying "recognized" instead of "created"?

   _____

   _____

   _____

   _____

2. Many writings that early Christians considered helpful and beneficial are *not* a part of the canon. What does this suggest about the New Testament books that *are* in the Bible?

   _____

   _____

   _____

   _____

3. Except for a few texts on the fringes of the canon, Christians throughout the world recognized the books of the New Testament as Scripture from the time they were written. How does this show God's faithfulness in giving us his Word? How should this affect our attitude toward the Bible and its impact in our lives?

   _____

   _____

   _____

   _____

   _____

   _____

   _____

Wrap It Up (5 MINUTES)

Prayer for the Road

"Father in heaven, by your grace, help us to grow in our understanding of your Word. In this journey, protect us from error in our own thoughts and the false teaching of others. Amen."

Application for Daily Life

The biblical authors often described the power God's Word to combat all sorts of evil, including deceitful teachings. As a group, dedicate yourselves to encouraging and pushing each other to memorize and study Scripture.

Encourage students to read *How We Got the Bible* handbook this week: "Chapter 5: Who Created the New Testament Canon?"

Questions Participants May Ask

Can every book in the New Testament be connected to an eyewitness?

Yes! See this helpful table:

Book	Author
Matthew	Matthew, apostle and eyewitness of the risen Lord (Matthew 9:9; 10:3; Acts 1:13)
Mark	Mark, traveling companion and translator for Simon Peter (1 Peter 1:13); "Mark, in his capacity as Peter's interpreter, wrote down accurately as much as he remembered." (Papias of Hierapolis, 2nd century)
Luke and Acts	Luke, traveling companion with Paul (Colossians 4:14; 2 Timothy 4:11); "Luke—the attendant of Paul—recorded in a book the Gospel that Paul declared." (Irenaeus of Lyon, 2nd century)
John	John, apostle and eyewitness of the risen Lord (Matthew 4:21; 10:2; Acts 1:13)
Romans, 1 and 2 Corinthians, Galatians, Ephesians, Philippians, Colossians, 1 and 2 Thessalonians, 1 and 2 Timothy, Titus, Philemon	Paul, apostle and later eyewitness of the risen Lord (1 Corinthians 9:1; 15:8–10). Some scholars deny that Paul authored some of these texts because of changes in the writing style; however, since Paul wrote these letters over a period of two decades and composed them with a secretary, a change in style does not necessarily indicate a change in authorship.
Hebrews	Received by early Christians as a proclamation from Paul or as a reliable reflection of Paul's theology written by someone else, based on the mention of Timothy (Hebrews 13:23). "Who wrote it, in truth, God only knows." (Origen of Alexandria, 3rd century)

Book	Author
James	James the Just, relative of Jesus and eyewitness of the risen Lord, recognized later as an apostle (Matthew 13:55; 1 Corinthians 15:7; Galatians 1:19; 2:9)
1 and 2 Peter	Peter, apostle and eyewitness of the risen Lord (Matthew 4:18; 10:2; Acts 1:13). Second Peter is so different from 1 Peter that many scholars deny that Simon Peter wrote 2 Peter. It is more likely that the shift between the two letters is due to different circumstances and different secretaries being involved in the composition of each letter.
1 John	John, apostle and eyewitness of the risen Lord (Matthew 4:21; 10:2; Acts 1:13)
2 and 3 John	John, apostle and eyewitness of the risen Lord (Matthew 4:21; 10:2; Acts 1:13); these epistles may have been written by another eyewitness named John, known as "John the elder," mentioned by Papias of Hierapolis (2nd century).
Jude	Jude, relative of Jesus and eyewitness of the risen Lord (Matthew 13:55)
Revelation	John, apostle and eyewitness of the risen Lord (Matthew 4:21; 10:2; Acts 1:13); it is possible, though unlikely, that Revelation was written by another eyewitness named John, known as "John the elder," mentioned by Papias of Hierapolis (2nd century).

Who created the New Testament canon?

No church council or bishop created the New Testament canon; instead, Christians recognized and received a canon that God created. This canon was breathed out by God as Christ-commissioned eyewitnesses and their close associates authored the books of the New Testament. A consensus emerged no later than the second century regarding the Gospels, Acts, the letters of Paul, and at least the first letter from John. By the end of the fourth century, Christians had concluded that 27 texts—the same texts found in your New Testament still today—could be traced back to apostolic eyewitnesses and their associates.

Michael Kruger has delineated three stages in the development of the canon:

The ontological canon: as soon as a God-inspired eyewitness or associate of an eyewitness wrote the words breathed out by God, this text was canon, whether or not everyone recognized it yet.

The functional canon: Texts were received as canon and functioned as canon in the churches. Occasionally, Christians in certain locations may have received a text as canon that wasn't really canonical at all—but it's important to recognize that the core books of the New Testament (the Gospels, Acts, Paul's letters, at least one letter from John) seem to have been received immediately and universally; there is no hint of any time when any of these texts was ever questioned.

The exclusive canon: When Athanasius of Alexandria sent out his Easter letter in AD 367, he was recognizing a consensus that had already emerged. Only 27 books could be traced back to apostolic eyewitnesses and their close associates and, therefore, only these 27 books should be recognized as New Testament canon.[29]

How can we know that Matthew, Mark, Luke and John were really the sources behind the Gospels?

Consistent and reliable traditions have connected the names of Matthew, Mark, Luke, and John with these Gospels from the first century onward. Some scholars claim that the New Testament Gospels received their names in the same way that some of the "lost Gospels" received their titles—people wanted these writings to seem authoritative; so, they simply added names of eyewitnesses, even though these people really didn't write the Gospels at all. However, the Gospels According to Matthew, Mark, Luke, and John seem to have been connected with their authors as soon as the Gospels began to circulate widely. Since some people who knew the authors would still have been alive; under these circumstances, it would have been difficult to ascribe false names to the Gospels without someone protesting.

Recommended Resources

1, 2 Peter, Jude, vol. 37 (*The New American Commentary*) by Thomas R. Schreiner (Nashville: Broadman & Holman Publishers, 2003)

The Canon of Scripture by F. F. Bruce (Downers Grove: IVP Academic, 1988)

Misquoting Truth by Timothy Paul Jones (InterVarsity Press, 2007)

Gospels, Lost and Found pamphlet by Timothy Paul Jones (Rose Publishing, 2007)

"How was it decided which books would be put in the Bible?" by Timothy Paul Jones (www.godtube.com/watch/?v=0J0C01NU)

Articles about the development of the New Testament canon (http://michaeljkruger.com/articles)

Notes:

_____

_____

_____

_____

_____

_____

_____

_____

_____

_____

_____

Notes:

How the New Testament Was Copied

Get This: God has preserved his Word sufficiently for us to recover the message he intended.

"The grass withers, the flower fades, but the word of our God will stand forever."—Isaiah 40:8

Session 5 Outline

Use this session outline to follow along with the video and take notes.

1. Early Christians cared deeply about maintaining the text.

    a. Warning not to add or take away words from Scripture (Revelation 22:18–19; 1st century AD)

    b. Origen of Alexandria rebuked scribes who changed the text of Scripture (3rd century AD)

    c. *Codex Vaticanus* shows a copyist chastising an earlier copyist who changed one of the readings of Scripture (4th century AD)

    d. Earliest Copies:

        i. Papyrus 52 - John 18 (2nd century AD)

        ii. Papyrus 104 - Matthew 21 (2nd century AD)

        iii. Possible fragment of Mark's Gospel (late 1st or early 2nd century AD)

        iv. Papyrus 66 and Papyrus 45 - John and Luke (about AD 200)

2. Overwhelming majority of variations have no impact on our translations.

   a. Example of a text variation: John 3:3 *Codex Sinaiticus*

   b. Most variations are things like a Greek definite article added or dropped out, a misspelling, or different word order that do not affect translation.

3. Textual criticism can recover nearly every original word.

   a. More than 5,600 New Testament fragments and manuscripts survive today.

   b. Examples of differences: John 5:4; Acts 8:37; Mark 16:8–20; John 7:53–8:11.

   c. 97–99% of the original text can be reconstructed.

4. Variations do not affect anything we believe about God or his work.

   a. Example: John 1:18, compare with John 20:28; 3:16. Jesus is both the Son and God.

Key Terms

Codex— (from Latin *caudex*, "block") The book form of ancient manuscripts, made up of a number of sheets of papyrus or parchment stacked and bound by fixing one edge. The codex was sometimes used by the Romans for business and legal transactions. Early Christians gathered the New Testament books in codex form.

Codex Sinaiticus—Codex Sinaiticus is a fourth-century Greek manuscript and generally considered to be one of the most important witnesses to the text because of its antiquity and clear concern for accuracy.

Codex Vaticanus—Codex Vaticanus is perhaps the oldest uncial manuscript and one of the most important witnesses to the text of the New Testament. It was probably copied no later than the middle of the fourth century.

Johannes Gutenberg (1397–1468)—Johannes Gutenberg, born in Mainz, Germany, is acknowledged as a key contributor to the invention of movable type printing. Gutenberg was seeking more rapid methods for producing books, which until then were produced slowly by copyists using quills and reeds or by printing with hand stamps and woodcuts. Gutenberg developed an oil-based ink and a typecasting machine that used a tin alloy to cast movable metal type. Using this method, a printer could make identical copies of a book quite quickly—about 300 copies per day.

Koine Greek—The common Greek language of the New Testament era, used by the authors of the New Testament.

Papyrus—A tall, aquatic reed that grows in the Nile Delta of Egypt and was made into a writing material of the same name. Papyrus was a primary writing surface throughout the Mediterranean world from the fourth century BC to the seventh century AD. The earliest surviving New Testament Greek manuscripts were written on papyrus.

Scribe—A person who copied ancient documents by hand as a profession. Scribes became less important with the invention of the printing press in the fifteenth century.

Textual Criticism—The scholarly discipline of establishing the text as near to the original as possible. Since we no longer have any original manuscripts, or "autographs," scholars must sort and evaluate the variant wordings of existing copies. The textual critic not only sorts through manuscripts and fragments for copyist errors but also considers early translations and lectionaries—church worship resources—to determine the original reading of each text.[30]

Uncial—Writing script commonly used in manuscripts from the 4th until the 8th century AD. Uncial scripts are written in majuscule (all upper-case letters). Many important manuscripts of the New Testament—including Codex Sinaiticus and Codex Vaticanus—were written in uncial script.

Variant—Copying differences between manuscripts.

Before the Gathering

- Prayerfully seek God's guidance for this gathering.

- **Watch the video:** *Session 5: How the New Testament Was Copied* (30 minutes)

- **Read the book:** Chapter 6 of *How We Got the Bible* handbook

- **Consider the questions:** Review the group discussion questions provided in this Leader Guide and choose 2 or 3 questions. Also, spend some time considering the *Questions Participants May Ask.*

- If opening the session with the infographic provided in this Leader Guide, print or copy the circles, then cut each one out. (See *Open the Session*)

- If you are expanding the session (optional):

  ○ Study the key Bible passage: John 1:18; 3:16; 20:28 (It will be beneficial if you look at the footnotes concerning these verses in a study Bible to become more familiar with the differences in biblical texts. See, for example, the footnotes in the ESV Study Bible or in the New King James Version).

  ○ Review the participant study questions—also provided here in the Leader Guide.

  ○ If you are using the PowerPoint® presentation, review the slides about the Latin Vulgate, the Masoretes, how the Bible was copied, and the materials on which the Bible was copied.

- Set up and test audio and video equipment beforehand.

Gathering Together

Open the Session (5 MINUTES)

Before class time, give four volunteers each one of the circles. To open the group time, ask the volunteer with Julius Caesar's *Gallic Wars* (the smallest circle) to read the number on their circle (10). Explain that this is the number of ancient manuscripts or fragments from this ancient text that survive today. Then do the same for Plato's *Tetralogies* (the next largest circle), then for Homer's *Iliad*. Finally, ask the person with the largest circle to read the number on their circle (5,600+).

Explain how there are more ancient New Testament manuscripts or fragments that survive today than any other ancient work. So how can we be confident that God's Word has been accurately preserved in these thousands of manuscripts? That's what this session will tell us. (This can also be done instead with different sized objects representing the different numbers of manuscripts: for example, a marble for Julius Caesar; a ping-pong ball or golf ball for Plato; a baseball or tennis ball for Homer; and a basketball or soccer ball for the New Testament.)

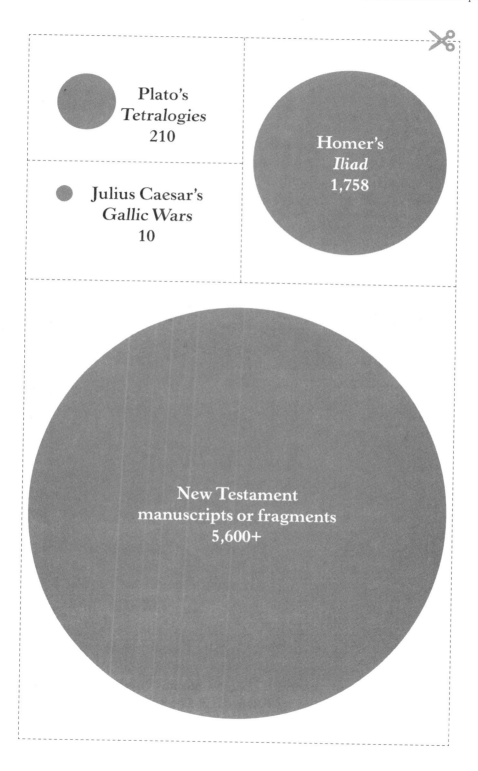

Plato's
Tetralogies
210

Julius Caesar's
Gallic Wars
10

Homer's
Iliad
1,758

New Testament
manuscripts or fragments
5,600+

Take a Closer Look (30 MINUTES)

Watch the video *Session 5: How the New Testament Was Copied*

Seek the Central Truth (30 MINUTES - OPTIONAL)

Key Bible Passage

Drawing from your personal study and from the study notes, guide participants in a discussion of John 1:14–18; 3:16; 20:28.

Study Notes:

The point of studying these three verses is to reinforce this truth: even if we don't know how to solve every textual variant perfectly, what we believe about God and his work in the world is not affected.

John 1:18 presents a textual difficulty. There are two primary possible readings:

1. Some Greek manuscripts support the translation "the only God" or "one and only God" (or "only begotten God"). If this manuscript variant is correct, the verse states that Jesus is God.
2. Other Greek manuscripts support the translation "the only Son" or "one and only Son" (or "only begotten Son").[31] If this manuscript variant is correct, the verse states that Jesus is the Son.

The words of Jesus through John in John 3:16 clearly affirm that Jesus is the Son of God.

On a tiny percentage of variants, scholars aren't absolutely certain of the original reading. Not one of these uncertainties affects what we believe about God or his work in the world. John 1:18 is one example, where the reading "one and only Son" or "one and only God" are both present in different translations. While both variants are possible, they both echo truths taught elsewhere in Scripture and both fit with what we are taught throughout John's Gospel!

- Thomas's confession in John 20:28 is one of the clearest affirmations in the New Testament that Jesus is fully God.

- The words of Jesus through John in John 3:16 clearly affirm that Jesus is the Son of God.

Nothing that we believe about Jesus is, therefore, changed because of the textual variant in John 1:18.

Study Questions:

1. John's Gospel is a book-length demonstration that God himself has been revealed in the flesh among humankind.[32] Look again at John 1:14–18. According to these verses, what was the purpose of Jesus' coming in the flesh?

    _____

    _____

    _____

2. According to John 1:14–18, what specific aspects of God's character are revealed through Jesus?

    _____

    _____

    _____

3. Thomas's confession in John 20:28 is a key moment in John's Gospel. What does this confession tell us about early Christian beliefs about Jesus?

    _____

    _____

    _____

PowerPoint® Presentation

Teach through the slides about the Latin Vulgate, the Masoretes, how the Bible was copied, and the materials on which the Bible was copied.

Get Them Talking (20 MINUTES)

Discuss two or more of these questions.

1. What do issues of translation and textual criticism teach us about God's faithfulness in preserving his Word?

_____

_____

_____

2. How does the truth of God's preservation of Scripture affect the way that you read the Bible?

_____

_____

_____

3. In this session, we have seen how deeply early Christians cared for Scripture and how important it was to them to faithfully pass on these sacred writings. In what ways do you see Christians today caring deeply for God Word?

_____

_____

_____

Are there areas where you see a lack of concern for God's Word?

_____

_____

Wrap It Up (5 MINUTES)

Prayer for the Road

"Father in heaven, thank you for sending your Son—Jesus Christ, God in flesh—that we might believe he is the Christ and have eternal life in his name. Help us always to have confidence in your Word. Build us in faith according to your grace. Amen."

Application for Daily Life

Scripture says that Jesus is the visible image of the invisible God. Take some extra time in your Bible study (personal or group study) to look through John's Gospel and write down what you learn about God by looking at Jesus.

Encourage students to read *How We Got the Bible* handbook this week: "How the Bible Made It from Manuscripts to You" and "Chapter 6: How Was the New Testament Copied?"

Questions Participants May Ask

Did copyists change texts to avoid difficulties?

The copyists were just as prone to imperfect attention spans, poor eyesight, fatigue and temptations to make unneeded changes as you or I might be. Occasionally, copyists did change or add words on purpose, usually to clarify something that seemed vague to them. The good news is that:

- The majority of copying differences make little or no difference when translated into English.

- Because there are so many manuscripts of the New Testament, scholars are almost always able to recognize and to correct changes by comparing multiple ancient manuscripts.

- Copyists were far more concerned with preserving sacred Scripture than with promoting their own agendas.

When copies of the New Testament vary, how do scholars determine which reading is the original?

So how do New Testament scholars choose the reading of a text that most probably represents the original writing, especially when there are several possibilities? Here are basic principles that most textual critics follow:

1. Look *beyond* the manuscript
   - at which reading is *oldest,*

   - at which reading is supported by texts that were separated by the *farthest distance*, and

   - to which *textual family* the manuscript belongs.[33] Each textual family (Western, Alexandrian, or Byzantine) represents a certain pattern of preservation and changes in the New Testament manuscripts. By comparing the families, textual critics are often able to determine *when* and *where* certain changes occurred.

2. Look within the manuscript for which reading is more probable based on
   - what a copyist would be most likely to change,

   - which possible reading is shortest,

   - which reading might have been an attempt to harmonize one text with another, and

- what difficult words a copyist might have replaced with simpler ones.

3. Look at *other writings* by the same original author to see which reading is most similar to the author's other writings.

How can I trust the Bible when I know about these copying mistakes?

In every case in which two or more options remain possible, every possible option simply reinforces truths that are already clearly present in the writings of that particular author and in the New Testament as a whole. There is no point at which any of the possible options would require readers to rethink an essential belief about Jesus or to doubt the historical integrity of the New Testament. Simply put, the differences are not highly significant.[34] The differences in manuscripts, whether accidental or intentional, in no way affect Christian faith and practice.

Recommended Resources

Misquoting Truth by Timothy Paul Jones (Downers Grove: InterVarsity, 2001)

The Gospel According to John (The Pillar New Testament Commentary) by D. A. Carson (Grand Rapids: Eerdmans, 1991)

The Center for the Study of New Testament Manuscripts (www.csntm.org)

Notes:

_____

_____

_____

_____

_____

_____

_____

_____

_____

_____

_____

_____

_____

_____

_____

_____

_____

_____

_____

Notes:

_____

_____

_____

_____

_____

_____

_____

_____

_____

_____

_____

_____

_____

_____

_____

_____

How We Got the Bible in English

Get This: Every person in every language needs a Bible that they can understand.

"Go therefore and make disciples of all nations, baptizing them in the name of the Father and of the Son and of the Holy Spirit."—Matthew 28:19–20

Session 6 Outline

Use this session outline to follow along with the video and take notes.

1. John Wycliffe

    a. He translated the Bible into English from Latin (1382).

    b. He was condemned (1415) and burned for heresy (1428) after he was dead.

    c. About a century after Wycliffe, Martin Luther translated the Bible into German (1534).

2. Three key events in the 1400s.

    a. Gutenberg printing press made mass printing possible (1455).

    b. Fall of Constantinople caused Eastern Christians to flee West with their Greek New Testaments (1453).

    c. Renaissance of interest in ancient languages emerged in European universities.

3. Greek New Testament

    a. Erasmus published Latin and Greek side by side (1516).

    b. Robert Stephanus (Estienne) introduced verse divisions.

    c. *Textus Receptus* (Received Text): Greek New Testaments traced back to Erasmus.

4. William Tyndale

a. He translated the Bible into English from Greek and Hebrew (1525–1535).

b. His translation influenced the Matthew's Bible (1537), the Great Bible (1539), and the Geneva Bible (1560).

5. King James Bible (1611)

a. Puritans petitioned King James for reform, including new English translation of the Bible.

b. King James Version became most popular English version.

6. Later English Translations

a. Older manuscripts discovered (18th–19th centuries)

b. English Revised Version (1885)/American Standard Version (1901)

c. Over 900 English translations

Key Terms

Erasmus of Rotterdam (c. 1466–1536)—A Dutch biblical scholar, philologist, and textual critic. Erasmus is credited with editing the first published edition of the Greek New Testament in 1516, a text that was revised several times in the following years. The translators of the King James Version relied on a later edition of the Greek text of Erasmus when they translated the New Testament.[35]

Geneva Bible (1560)—The Bible used by William Shakespeare, the Geneva Bible, was translated by Protestant refugees from England during the reign of Queen Mary I ("Bloody Mary"). Much of the translation was shaped by the Great Bible and Tyndale's New Testament.

Great Bible (1539)—Myles Coverdale based this Bible on the Matthew's Version. A copy of the Great Bible was placed in every church in England.

King James Version (1611)—A title used for the English translation of the Bible commonly known as the Authorized Version. Translated at the command of King James I of England. It was revised several times. The 1769 edition is the version used most widely today.

Matthew's Version—John Rogers brought together Tyndale's published and unpublished translations with Coverdale's translation of the Old Testament Prophets (as well as the Apocrypha). Published under the pseudonym "Thomas Matthew."

Robert Stephanus (Estienne)—Editor of the Stephanus Greek New Testaments; divided biblical chapters into verses in one of his early Greek New Testaments.

Textus Receptus—Latin for "received text." Refers to the entire series of published Greek New Testaments that derive from Erasmus' text.[36]

William Tyndale (c. 1494–1536)—A translator of the Bible, known as "the father of the English Bible." He sometimes used the pseudonym William Huchyns. Around 1522, he conceived the project of translating the Bible into English, but had to relocate to Germany to be free to do so. The printing of his first translation of the New Testament was interrupted by the local authorities but eventually completed later that year. On its arrival in England in 1526, it was bitterly attacked by local archbishops. Tyndale spent most of his remaining years at Antwerp, Belgium, where he frequently revised the New Testament. His biblical translations, made direct from the Greek and Hebrew into straightforward and vigorous English, have influenced virtually every subsequent English translation. In 1535 he was arrested, imprisoned, strangled, and burnt at the stake.[37]

John Wycliffe (c. 1330–1384)—English philosopher, theologian, and reformer. Wycliffe held that people need the Bible in their native language. It is uncertain whether Wycliffe took any direct part in the translation of the first entirely English Bible, but most scholars attribute to Wycliffe either oversight or inspiration of the project that eventually became known as the Wycliffe Bible.

Vulgate—The Latin translation of the Bible by Jerome in the fourth century AD (Latin *vulgo,* "to make common, accessible"). It is characterized by its adherence to the Hebrew text of the Old Testament rather than reliance on the Septuagint or some other translation. The Wycliffe Bible began as an almost word-for-word translation of the Latin Vulgate.[38]

Before the Gathering

- Prayerfully seek God's guidance for this gathering.

- **Watch the video:** *Session 6: How We Got the Bible in English* (30 minutes)

- **Read the book:** Chapter 7 of *How We Got the Bible* handbook

- **Consider the questions:** Review the group discussion questions provided in this Leader Guide and choose 2 or 3 questions. Also, spend some time considering the *Questions Participants May Ask.*

- If opening the session with the "Who am I?" activity (see *Open the Session*) and ending the session with retaking the quiz from the first meeting, be sure to allow time for both. You may need to reduce the group discussion time by a few minutes.

- If you are expanding the session (optional):

    ○ Study the key Bible passage: Matthew 28:19

    ○ Review the participant study questions—also provided here in the Leader Guide.

    ○ If you are using the PowerPoint® presentation, review the slides on the history of the English Bible. If there's time, consider also taking your class through the section "English Bible Translations Today."

- Set up and test audio and video equipment beforehand.

Gathering Together

Opening the Session (5–10 MINUTES)

Play a quick game of "Who am I?" Of course it's not really a game—no teams or keeping score. It's just a fun way to introduce participants to this session's material. Hand four volunteers each one of the "Who am I?" cards. Have the person with card number 1 read his or her card (but not the answer at the bottom) and have the class try to guess the answer. If no one in the class knows the answer, have the reader with the card reveal the correct answer. Then do the same with cards 2 through 4. If nobody in the class knows the answers, it's OK; remind participants that they *will* know the answers after this session.

Take a Closer Look (30 MINUTES)

Watch the video *Session 6: How We Got the Bible in English*

Seek the Central Truth (30 MINUTES - OPTIONAL)

Key Bible Passage

Drawing from your personal study and from the study notes, guide participants in a discussion of Matthew 28:19–20.

Study Notes:

"Make disciples" is a command. Going, baptizing, and teaching are the means by which we are to obey Jesus's command.

The Gospel According to Matthew began with the prophecy that Jesus would be called Immanuel, which means "God with us" (1:23). The book ends with Jesus promising that he is indeed with us until the end of the age (28:20).

1 I finally gave in to those pesky Puritans always trying to purify the Church of England! As king, I granted their request for a new English translation of the Bible. It was completed in 1611, and, thankfully, it got rid of those notes in the margins of earlier Bibles that seemed to question my authority as king. Who am I?

ANSWER: *King James I of England*

2 I oversaw a translation of the Bible into English from Latin. Some church leaders accused me of making the Bible "common to all… even to women!" I was accused of heresy over and over again. Though I died, still officially in good standing with the church, they wouldn't let it go. After I had been dead for decades, they dug up my bones and burned them at the stake. Who am I?

ANSWER: *John Wycliffe*

3 I wanted everyone to see how closely my corrected Latin New Testament followed the original Greek. So I placed the Greek New Testament in one column and my Latin version in the other column. Ironically, history now remembers me, not for my excellent Latin version, but that I ended up producing the first published Greek New Testament. Who am I?

ANSWER: *Erasmus of Rotterdam*

4 I translated the New Testament into English because I believed that everyone—from the king to the plowboy—should have a Bible they can understand. My translations have shaped almost every later English translation of the Bible. Unfortunately, I ended up on the wrong side of a king, and I was strangled and burned to death. My dying words were, "Lord, open the king of England's eyes!" Who am I?

ANSWER: *William Tyndale*

Study Questions:

1. How does the Great Commission connect to the history of the English Bible?

    _____

    _____

    _____

    _____

    _____

2. In particular, how does the Great Commission connect to the work of John Wycliffe and William Tyndale?

    _____

    _____

    _____

    _____

    _____

3. Why do we need the Scriptures to be able to make disciples in every nation?

    _____

    _____

    _____

    _____

    _____

PowerPoint® Presentation

Teach through slides about the history of the English Bible and the section "English Bible Translations Today."

Get Them Talking (15–20 MINUTES)

Discuss two or more of these questions.

1. If you could meet John Wycliffe or William Tyndale today, what would you say to them?

   _____

   _____

   _____

   _____

   _____

   _____

2. Do you think it is helpful to have so many different English translations today? Explain why or why not.

   _____

   _____

   _____

   _____

3. How should knowing that people died for their efforts to get the Bible translated into other languages impact your Bible study, prayer, and worship?

   _____

   _____

   _____

   _____

4. Nearly 2,000 people groups have no Bible in their language. What should be our priority as we consider how to make disciples in these people groups?

   _____

   _____

   _____

Wrap It Up (5–10 MINUTES)

See What You Learned

Have participants take the same quiz that they took in the first session. Then read the correct answers aloud (see *Answer Key*) and let participants score their own quizzes. You can also give them back their original quizzes that they took in Session 1 so they can see how much they've learned since starting this study. If you did not give the quiz in the first session, you can still use the quiz here. The quiz covers material from all six sessions.

Prayer for the Road

"Father in heaven, may your Word continue to spread to the ends of the earth and make disciples wherever it is read, preached, and heard. Give us hearts to be a part of this great work, Lord. Amen."

Application for Daily Life

Plan a group (or church) activity designed to get Bibles to people who need them. This could be done at a local level, a global level, or both! Perhaps you could plan a garage sale or some similar event to raise money to purchase new Bibles to send overseas or to local missions. God's Word is essential to the making of disciples. As a group, work together to make certain that everyone everywhere has access to the Scriptures.

Encourage students to read *How We Got the Bible* handbook this week: "Chapter 7: Where Did the English Bible Come From?"

> "Just as William Tyndale prayed, 'Lord, open the king of England's eyes,' perhaps our prayer should be today, 'Lord, open our eyes to the need around us,' to train translators and to send translators so that we provide the world with the Word of God."—Timothy Paul Jones

How We Got the Bible Quiz

1. How many books are in the Bible?

    _____

2. How many human authors wrote the books of the Bible?

    a. Fewer than 10

    b. Between 10 and 25

    c. At least 40

    d. More than 100

3. What do we call the original manuscripts of the Bible?

    _____

4. How many original manuscripts of the Bible survive today?

    _____

5. In what language(s) was the Old Testament originally written?

    _____

6. In what language was the New Testament originally written?

    _____

7. What do we call the ancient Greek translation of the Old Testament?

   _____

8. When did mass printing of Bibles begin?

   a. Before AD 300

   b. Around AD 650

   c. After AD 1400

   d. After AD 1750

9. How many ancient Greek manuscripts of the New Testament exist?

   a. Fewer than 1,000

   b. Between 1,000 and 2,500

   c. Between 2,500 and 5,000

   d. More than 5,000

10. Who is known as the "father of the English Bible"?

    _____

Answer Key:

(1) 66

(2) c. At least 40

(3) Autographs

(4) Zero. There are no surviving *original* manuscripts.

(5) Hebrew (and some portions in Aramaic)

(6) Greek (or Koine Greek)

(7) Septuagint (or LXX)

(8) c. After AD 1400 (Gutenberg Printing Press about AD 1450)

(9) d. More than 5,000

(10) William Tyndale (John Wycliffe could also be a correct response.)

Questions Participants May Ask

How did the King James Version come about?

King James I of England ordered that work on a new translation be begun, and a strong body of revisers was formed. The scholars were instructed to take the Bishops Bible as their basis, to consult all earlier versions, to retain traditional terms (such "church" and "baptism"), and to exclude all marginal notes, unless required to explain some Hebrew or Greek word. Each group worked separately at first, with a specific portion of the Bible assigned to the scholars in that group. They then sent their work to the others for criticism; final decisions were made at a general meeting of the chief members of each group, with scholars from outside being called in to discuss special difficulties. William Tyndale's influence through various versions down to the Bishops Bible fixed the general tone of the translation. The work, begun in 1607, took two years and nine months to prepare for the press and first appeared in large folio volumes in 1611. The "Preface of the Translators" explains that it is a revision, not a new translation, and that the revisers, who had the original Hebrew and Greek texts before them, steered a course between the Puritan and Roman Catholic versions. On the title page are the words "appointed to be read in churches."[39]

Is there a best version of the English Bible?

The "best version" sometimes depends on the needs of the reader.

- Functional equivalent translations follow the original text phrase-by-phrase instead of word-by-word. For newer Christians or persons for whom English is a second language, a functional equivalent version like the New Living Translation might be the best place to start.

- Formal equivalent translations strive to follow the wording of the Hebrew, Aramaic, and Greek texts as closely as possible; for mature Christians or for in-depth study, formal equivalent translations like the English Standard Version or the New American Standard Bible may be more appropriate.

- A few translations—like the Holman Christian Standard Bible, the NET Bible, and God's Word—try to balance functional and formal equivalence.

In truth, however, God can work through almost any translation of the Bible, as long as the translation seeks to state the meaning of the original texts in a new language instead of tweaking the meaning to fit a certain political or theological agenda.

Recommended Resources

The Daring Mission of William Tyndale by Steven J. Lawson (Sanford: Reformation Trust, 2015)

Matthew (The NIV Application Commentary) by Michael J. Wilkins (Grand Rapids: Zondervan, 2004)

Virtual tour of the Dunham Bible Museum: www.hbu.edu/About-HBU/ The-Campus/Facilities/Morris-Cultural-Arts-Center/Museums/Dunham-Bible-Museum/Tour-of-the-Museum.aspx

Statistics on the status of worldwide Bible translation efforts: www.wycliffe.net

Notes:

_____

_____

_____

_____

_____

_____

_____

_____

_____

_____

_____

_____

Class Feedback

What was your favorite thing about this Bible study, and why?

_____

_____

_____

How could the meeting location, setting, length, or time be improved?

_____

_____

_____

Do you think the material covered was too difficult, too easy, or just about right?

_____

_____

_____

What would you like to see different about the group discussions, activities, or anything else about the class?

_____

_____

_____

What topic(s) would you suggest for the next Bible study?

_____

_____

_____

(Notes)

[1] Stanley Grenz, David Guretzki, and Cherith Fee Nordling, *Pocket Dictionary of Theological Terms* (Downers Grove, IL: InterVarsity Press, 1999), 62.

[2] Clement of Rome, *Letter to the Corinthians*, 45.

[3] Irenaeus, *Against Heresies*, 2:28:3.

[4] Justin Martyr, *Dialogue with Trypho*, 65.

[5] Tertullian of Carthage, *Treatise on the Soul*, 21.

[6] Athanasius of Alexandria, *Easter Letter*, 19:3.

[7] Augustine of Hippo, *Letters*, 82.

[8] Arthur G. Patzia and Anthony J. Petrotta, *Pocket Dictionary of Biblical Studies* (Downers Grove, IL: InterVarsity Press, 2002), 13–14.

[9] Patzia and Petrotta, *Pocket Dictionary*, 22.

[10] Patzia and Petrotta, *Pocket Dictionary*, 32–33.

[11] F. L. Cross and Elizabeth A. Livingstone, eds., *The Oxford Dictionary of the Christian Church* (Oxford; New York: Oxford University Press, 2005), 872.

[12] Patzia and Petrotta, *Pocket Dictionary*, 69.

[13] Patzia and Petrotta, *Pocket Dictionary*, 77.

[14] Patzia and Petrotta, *Pocket Dictionary*, 84.

[15] Patzia and Petrotta, *Pocket Dictionary*, 105.

[16] Mervin Breneman, *Ezra, Nehemiah, Esther,* electronic ed., vol. 10, *The New American Commentary* (Nashville: Broadman & Holman Publishers, 1993), 227.

[17] Definition draws from multiple sources including Tim Keller, "Vision and Values": http://www.redeemer.com, and, Scot McKnight, Embracing Grace (Brewster: Paraclete, 2005), 12.

[18] Richard Burridge, *What Are the Gospels?* 2nd ed. (Grand Rapids: Eerdmans, 2004) makes a definitive case that the New Testament Gospels fit into the broader category of the Greco-Roman *bios.* That said, the Gospel-writers' understanding of Gospels as a continuation of a storyline that God began in the Old Testament and of Jesus as the antitype of Old Testament characters contributed to the composition of the Gospels as a unique subtype of bios. For further exploration of this topic, see chapter 2 in Jonathan Pennington, *Reading the Gospels Wisely* (Grand Rapids: Baker, 2012). On the historiographic nature of the Gospels and limitation of "Gospel" to texts which present the "gospel," see Michael Bird, *The Gospel of the Lord* (Grand Rapids: Eerdmans, 2014), 48-56, 289.

[19] Martin Luther, *Luther's Works XXVIII: Commentaries on 1 Corinthians 7 and 15.*

[20] David E. Garland, *1 Corinthians, Baker Exegetical Commentary on the New Testament* (Grand Rapids, MI: Baker Academic, 2003), 679.

[21] Ted Cabal et al., *The Apologetics Study Bible: Real Questions, Straight Answers, Stronger Faith* (Nashville, TN: Holman Bible Publishers, 2007), 1731.

[22] David E. Garland, 1 Corinthians, *Baker Exegetical Commentary on the New Testament* (Grand Rapids, MI: Baker Academic, 2003), 683.

[23] Tertullian, *Prescription Against Heretics*, 36.

[24] Daniel C. Arichea and Howard Hatton, *A Handbook on the Letter from Jude and the Second Letter from Peter, UBS Handbook Series* (New York: United Bible Societies, 1993), 66.

[25] Arichea and Hatton, *A Handbook on the Letter*, 66.

[26] Thomas R. Schreiner, *1, 2 Peter, Jude,* vol. 37, *The New American Commentary* (Nashville: Broadman & Holman Publishers, 2003), 395.

[27] Arichea and Hatton, *A Handbook on the Letter*, 163.

[28] Arichea and Hatton, *A Handbook on the Letter*, 164.

[29] Michael Kruger, *The Question of Canon* (Downers Grove: IVP, 2013).

[30] Patzia and Petrotta, *Pocket Dictionary*, 114–115.

[31] Barclay Moon Newman and Eugene Albert Nida, *A Handbook on the Gospel of John, UBS Handbook Series* (New York: United Bible Societies, 1993), 27.

[32] Herman Ridderbos, *The Gospel of John: A Theological Commentary* (Grand Rapids: Eerdmans, 1997), 49.

[33] For a brief explanation of the three textual families, see *Misquoting Truth* by Timothy Paul Jones (InterVarsity, 2007), 69.

[34] Jones, *Misquoting Truth*, 55.

[35] Patzia and Petrotta, *Pocket Dictionary,* 43.

[36] Patzia and Petrotta, *Pocket Dictionary*, 115.

[37] Cross and Livingstone, *The Oxford Dictionary of the Christian Church*, 1660.

[38] Patzia and Petrotta, *Pocket Dictionary*, 122.

[39] Cross and Livingstone, *The Oxford Dictionary of the Christian Church*, 136.

Other DVD-Based Studies For Individuals or Group Use

Christian History Made Easy
People and Events Every Christian Should Know

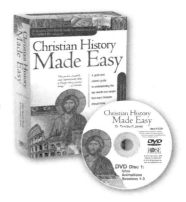

In this 12-session DVD-based study, Dr. Timothy Paul Jones takes you through the most important events in Christian history from the time of the apostles to today. He brings to life the fascinating people and events that shaped our world. This isn't dry names and dates. It's full of dramatic stories told with a touch of humor. This series, based on Dr. Jones's popular award-winning book Christian History Made Easy, ties in spiritual lessons believers can glean by looking at the past, and shows how God was still working in his church despite all the ups and downs.

157X Complete Kit 9781596365254
157DV ....Leader Pack 9781596365261
158X Leaders Guide... 9781596365278
159X Participants Guide.. 9781596365285
705X Book.. 9781596363281

Four Views of the End Times
Cut through the confusion about the *Book of Revelation*

What does the Bible actually say about the end times that lead to the return of Jesus Christ? The differing ideas that divide believers into four major points-of-view are examined in this Four Views of the End Times DVD-based small group study. This new six-session study shows four different Revelation time lines and tackles Dispensational Premillennialism, Postmillennialism, Historic Premillennialism, and Amillennialism. For each view, the objective study includes simple definitions, explanation and discussion of supporting Scriptures, an overview of the view's popularity, and a focus on what we can gain from studying this perspective, and common questions and answers.

770X Complete Kit 9781596364127
770DV ....Leader Pack 9781596364240
782X Leader Guide: Four Views 9781596364257
783X Participants Guide: Four Views............................ 9781596364264
350X Four Views of the End Times pamphlet................... 9781596360891

Feasts of the Bible
Connect the Hebrew roots of Christianity and the symbolism within each feast

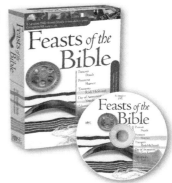

Some Christians miss the importance of the biblical feasts, seeing them as merely "Jewish" holidays, but Scripture says these are the Feasts of the Lord God, established for all people for all time. Now you can connect the Hebrew roots of Christianity and the symbolism within each feast that points to Jesus Christ. The Feasts and Holidays of the Bible will also show you how to conduct your own Christian Passover Seder, where you will learn how all the Old Testament Passover activities point symbolically to Jesus.

101X Complete Kit 9781596364646
101DV ....Leader Pack 9781596364653
102X Leaders Guide... 9781596364660
103X Participants Guide.. 9781596364677
455X Feasts of the Bible pamphlet................................ 9781890947583
108X Messiah in the Feasts of Israel book..................... 9780970261977